11/17

WORLD OF WORK

LAW & PUBLIC SAFETY

Exploring Career Pathways

Diane Lindsey Reeves & Lacey Reeves

Created and produced by
Bright Futures Press, Cary, North Carolina
www.brightfuturespress.com

Published by
Cherry Lake Publishing, Ann Arbor, Michigan
www.cherrylakepublishing.com

Photo Credits: Cover, Beautyline; page 7, 8, Lisa S.; page 7, 10, Fer Gregory; page 7, 12, Federal Bureau of Investigations; page 7, 14, Federal Bureau of Investigations; page 7, 16, Four Oaks; page 7, 18, ESB Professional; page 7, 20, John Roman Images; page 7, 22, Monkey Business Images; page 24, Billion Photos.

Library of Congress Cataloging-in-Publication Data

Names: Reeves, Diane Lindsey, 1959- author. I Reeves, Lacey, author.
Title: Law & public safety / Diane Lindsey Reeves, Lacey Reeves.
Other titles: Law and public safety
Description: Ann Arbor, Michigan : Cherry Lake Publishing, [2017] I Series:
    World of work I Includes bibliographical references and index.
Identifiers: LCCN 2016042182I ISBN 9781634726269 (hardcover) I ISBN
    9781634726368 (pdf) I ISBN 9781634726467 (pbk.) I ISBN 9781634726566
    (ebook)
Subjects: LCSH: Police--Vocational guidance--United States--Juvenile
    literature. I Public safety--Vocational guidance--United States--Juvenile
    literature.
Classification: LCC KF5398.P6 R44 2017 I DDC 364.973023--dc23
LC record available at https://lccn.loc.gov/2016042182

Printed in the United States of America.

TABLE OF CONTENTS

HELLO WORLD OF WORK

This is you.

Right now, your job is to go to school and learn all you can.

This is the world of work.

It's where people earn a living, find purpose in their lives, and make the world a better place.

Sooner or later, you'll have to find your way from

HERE to THERE.

To get started, take all the jobs in the incredibly enormous world of work and organize them into an imaginary pile. It's a big pile, isn't it? It would be pretty tricky to find the perfect job for you among so many options.

No worries!

Some very smart career experts have made it easier to figure out. They sorted jobs and industries into groups by the types of skills and products they share. These groups are called career clusters. They provide pathways that will make it easier for you to find career options that match your interests.

Architecture & Construction

Arts & Communications

Business & Administration

Education & Training

Finance

Food & Natural Resources

Government

Health Sciences

Hospitality & Tourism

Human Services

Information Technology

Law & Public Safety

Manufacturing

Marketing

Science, Technology, Engineering & Mathematics (STEM)

Transportation

Good thing you are still a kid.

You have lots of time to explore ideas and imagine yourself doing all kinds of amazing things. The **World of Work** (WoW for short) series of books will help you get started.

TAKE A HIKE!

There are 16 career pathways waiting for you to explore. The only question is: Which one should you explore first?

Is **Law** and **Public Safety** a good path for you to start exploring career ideas? There is a lot to admire about careers along this pathway. Among these professionals are first responders and other heroes who come to the rescue when bad things happen. They make the world a safer place and do all they can to make sure that liberty and justice continue in America.

See if any of the following questions grab your interest.

WOULD YOU ENJOY working on the school safety patrol, participating in a mock court trial at school, or coming up with a fire escape plan for your home?

CAN YOU IMAGINE someday working at a cyber security company, fire station, police department, or prison?

ARE YOU CURIOUS ABOUT what animal control officers, coroners, detectives, firefighters, or park rangers do?

If so, it's time to take a hike! Keep reading to see what kinds of opportunities you can discover along the Law and Public Safety pathway.

But wait!

What if you don't think you'll like this pathway?

You have two choices.

You could keep reading, to find out more than you already know. You might be surprised to learn how many amazing careers you'll find along this path.

OR

Turn to page 27 to get ideas about other WoW pathways.

FIREFIGHTER

ATTORNEY

PARALEGAL

WoW Up Close

Fight crime and put out fires. Uphold the law, prosecute criminal cases, and defend the accused. Investigate crimes and guard people and property. These are just some of the important jobs that people who work along the Law and Public Safety pathway do.

SOCIAL WORKER

POLICE OFFICER

SCENE DO NOT

CRIME SCENE INVESTIGATOR

FBI SPECIAL AGENT

EMERGENCY MANAGEMENT COORDINATOR

ATTORNEY

When most people think of an **attorney**, they picture a courtroom drama unfolding. Someone is accused of a crime. The prosecutor presents a case that tries to prove this person did what he or she is accused of doing. The defense argues that this person didn't do it. In the end, a **verdict** is reached and justice is (usually) served.

Some attorneys do this kind of work. But there are many other kinds of situations attorneys handle. Some attorneys **mediate** disputes such as divorces. Others represent businesses in deals, **negotiations**, and **lawsuits**. But there are many other kinds of situations attorneys handle. All attorneys must interpret the laws and represent their clients' interests to the best of their abilities.

Choosing what kind of law to practice depends on what kind of talents you have and how you want to spend your time. If you like to argue and are good at debating, you might make a good defense attorney. If you are interested in business, then real estate or corporate law may be a good fit.

Becoming an attorney requires extensive education and preparation. It starts with earning a four-year college degree. This is followed by three years of law school. Attorneys must pass a **bar exam** in the state where they want to work before they are allowed to practice law.

Check It Out!

Learn more about the laws of the land at

- ▶ https://www.icivics.org/games
- ▶ https://www.brainpop.com/games/lawcraft

Start Now!

- ✔ Join your school's debate team.
- ✔ Write for the school newspaper to practice your writing skills.
- ✔ Serve as a peer mediator at school to help resolve conflicts among classmates.

CRIME SCENE INVESTIGATER

Crime scenes are where mysteries meet science. When a crime happens, **crime scene investigators** (CSIs) use a mix of detective skills and science know-how to find out "whodunit." They scour crime scenes for the tiniest clues. Think: a strand of hair. Tiny pieces of broken glass. **DNA** samples on clothing.

Crime scene investigators identify the evidence and analyze it to eliminate suspects and build a case. Sometimes CSIs work on-site at an actual crime scene. Other times they work in the laboratory where they use really cool equipment to examine the evidence. Unlike TV where crimes are solved in an hour or less, it can take months or years to solve a crime. Crime scene investigators are also called on to **testify** as expert witnesses in court.

Becoming a crime scene investigator takes hard work and a serious commitment. A bachelor's degree in criminal justice, political science, biology, chemistry, or forensics is the first step. Experience in law enforcement and attending the police academy are often necessary too. After completing these requirements, on-the-job training comes next. Working under the supervision of a senior crime scene investigator helps to build skills and prepare future CSIs to take a certification exam.

Check It Out!

See crime scene investigators in action at

- ▶ http://on.natgeo.com/2dTh8Tv
- ▶ http://bit.ly/2dTScRc

Start Now!

- ✓ Binge on crime scene shows like *Bones*, *Elementary*, or *CSI*.
- ✓ Test your powers of deduction by playing a game of *Clue* with your friends.
- ✓ Use the Internet and library resources to find out how to "dust for fingerprints."

EMERGENCY
MANAGEMENT
COORDINATOR

A hurricane strikes and thousands of people must evacuate their homes. A bomb threat is made at a community center, and the rush to get outside is intense. In both cases, people could get and property could get damaged. The potential for **chaos** is great.

Thanks to the work of **emergency management coordinators**, **disaster** situations get quick and organized responses. Well-trained first responders know what to do and where to go. Emergency command centers are up and running in no time. Alerts to inform citizens are blasted through TV, radio, and e-mails. Hospitals and other medical providers are on emergency standby.

These kinds of responses come from careful planning and lots of practice *before* trouble hits. This job is all about imagining the what-ifs and coming up with solutions. What if a hurricane knocked out power to thousands of homes? What if roads had to be closed due to flooding? What is the best way to help people deal with the aftermath of an earthquake?

Most emergency management coordinators work for state or local governments. Others work for hospitals, universities, corporations, or the federal government. Future emergency management coordinators need a college degree in a subject like public administration, emergency management, or disaster planning.

Check It Out!

Find tips for how to prepare for emergencies at

▶ https://www.ready.gov/kids

▶ http://www.redcross.org/monsterguard

Start Now!

✓ Consider joining your local Scout troop where you'll learn valuable life skills.

✓ Make sure your family has emergency plans in place for fire, bad weather, and other potential big problems.

✓ Help your family put together an emergency kit with flashlights, batteries, first aid supplies, and other essentials.

FBI SPECIAL AGENT

FBI special agents have exciting jobs. They tackle some of America's most serious problems. Preventing terrorist attacks. Protecting the **civil rights** of citizens. Fighting against corruption. These are among the many responsibilities of the FBI.

There are various specialty units in the FBI, including domestic and international terrorism, foreign **counterintelligence**, and **cybercrime**. FBI agents are also tasked with solving very challenging crimes. If a serious crime happens in a community, local police may immediately call the FBI for backup in the investigation. FBI agents have special training and access to resources that can aid local law enforcement agencies.

As you probably guessed, not just anybody can become an FBI special agent. This is a highly competitive field that requires intense training—and, of course, rigorous background checks and a spotless record. You must be between the ages of 23 and 37 to be eligible for the FBI. A bachelor's degree in a relevant field is required. Training takes place at FBI headquarters and includes special investigative techniques, self-defense courses, and assessment skills. Ongoing training and education are encouraged for promotion and advancement.

Check It Out!

Learn more about the FBI at

▶ http://bit.ly/FBIKids

▶ http://bit.ly/FBIAcademy

Start Now!

✓ Join a school or community club and take on a leadership role.

✓ Take a self-defense or karate class.

FIREFIGHTER

Rushing into a burning building to save a baby or pet. Arriving at the scene of a car accident and rescuing a family trapped inside. It's just another day in the life of a **firefighter**. These real-life superheroes are among the bravest men and women in their communities.

Firefighters must be prepared for anything as they are often the first on scene at emergencies and fires. They put in long and unusual hours, working several days in a row away from home. Not every day brings danger and excitement, though. Many days are spent training and doing chores around the firehouse. Firefighters often play an important part in providing fire safety education in schools and at community events. They also work with fire inspectors to ensure that buildings are well equipped for an emergency situation.

It will probably come as no surprise that firefighters must in excellent physical shape. Volunteering at a fire station is the first step to becoming a firefighter. This will give you a taste for what being a firefighter is really like and help you determine if it's right for you. The requirements to become a firefighter vary from state to state, but some form of special training is necessary. Options include attending a firefighter academy, technical school, or college.

Check It Out!

Become an expert in fire safety at

- http://www.firesafekids.org
- http://www.firefacts.org

Start Now!

- Stop by your local firehouse for a tour from the firefighters.
- Learn everything you can about fire prevention and safety.
- Start pumping iron and get in shape.

PARALEGAL

Behind every good lawyer, you'll often find a **paralegal**. A lot of work goes into every court case, **legal brief**, and **contract**. Paralegals work alongside attorneys to manage their caseloads by doing much of the important behind-the-scenes work and research.

Investigative work, filing documents, and researching case law are just a few of a paralegal's responsibilities. Paralegals are also in charge of scheduling appointments with witnesses, clients, or other attorneys. Paralegals do many of the same sorts of things that lawyers do. However, there is a big difference. Paralegals cannot give legal advice. You won't see paralegals defending or prosecuting clients in court. But you may find them sitting next to the lawyer who does, providing documents and other support to help win the case.

Like attorneys, paralegals specialize in a variety of areas. Options include working for state or federal governments, large corporations, or private legal firms. Responsibilities vary greatly depending on which option is chosen.

Another difference between lawyers and paralegals is education. It takes at least 7 years of college and law school to become a lawyer. Paralegals can prepare with either a two-year associate's degree in paralegal studies or by attending special paralegal training after earning a four-year college degree.

Check It Out!

Find out more about what paralegals do at

 http://bit.ly/2dJ8wCy

http://bit.ly/2cY4EsF

Start Now!

- Join the school newspaper to build your writing skills and learn to work on a deadline.

- Create a filing system at home to organize your school assignments.

- Join a school club and volunteer to serve as the group secretary.

POLICE OFFICER

Laws are rules made by government to protect citizens. It is up to **police officers** to enforce these laws and keep communities safe from those who break the law.

Besides keeping dangerous criminals off the streets, police work as highway patrol officers to keep the roadways safe. This includes enforcing speed limits and ensuring that motorists are driving safely. Police are also often the first to respond to car crashes and other roadside emergencies. When a natural disaster strikes, police work with the military and government officials to help maintain order.

Of course, there's more to being a police officer than what you see on TV crime shows. There is plenty of paperwork involved, along with other administrative tasks. Police officers also have a duty to set a good example in their communities.

Police work is physically demanding, so officers must be in tip-top physical shape. A high school diploma is required, and a college degree is recommended for those who want to move up the ranks. An extensive background check is required to make sure that only the best candidates become officers. The screening process is followed by six months of special training in a policy academy.

Check It Out!

Explore what it's like to be a police officer at

- http://bit.ly/23b0c2y
- http://bit.ly/2dWtWtv
- http://bit.ly/2d7rWjk

Start Now!

- ✓ Join your school's safety patrol and volunteer to serve as a hall monitor.

- ✓ Try out a local self-defense class to learn valuable maneuvers.

- ✓ Check out "first responder workouts" online to get in shape police officer–style.

SOCIAL WORKER

When you see somebody in trouble, is your first instinct to lend a helping hand? If you enjoy helping others, a career as a **social worker** lets you put your passion to work. Social workers wear many hats and work in hospitals, adoption agencies, child welfare organizations, nursing homes, and private practice.

Family social workers work with families dealing with poverty, homelessness, and other hardships. They help families find assistance for food, housing, and other necessities. When parents struggle to provide safe and loving homes for their children, social workers help find caring foster homes for the children. Then they make sure parents get the support they need to get back on track, so that they can be reunited with their children.

Some social workers specialize in working with the elderly. They are called **geriatric** social workers, and they help aging people cope with financial, medical, and social problems. Medical social workers work in hospitals as case managers, patient navigators, and therapists. Clinical social workers diagnose and treat people with mental health issues and illnesses.

Volunteering is a good way to get ready for a job like this. The next step is to earn a college degree in social work or a related subject. To be competitive in this field, you may find a master's degree in social work helpful as well.

Check It Out!

See what social work is all about at

▶ http://bit.ly/SocialWork1

▶ http://bit.ly/SocialWork2

Start Now!

✓ Volunteer to help out at a local nursing home for older people, a religious training class for kids, or a community food bank.

✓ Organize a "fill the backpack" event for your class, to donate school supplies to children who need them.

911 dispatcher • Adjudicator • Administrative judge • Alcohol law enforcement agent • Alternative dispute resolution coordinator • Animal attendant • Animal control officer • Appeals examiner • Arbitrator • Arson investigator • **ATTORNEY** • Attorney general • Bailiff • Canine deputy • Canine (K-9) enforcement officer • Case manager • Chief of police • Child protective services caseworker • Civil process server • Communications officer • Correctional officer • Court reporter • Court security officer • Crew boss • Crime scene analyst • Crime scene evidence technician • **CRIME SCENE**

WoW Big List

Take a look at some of the different kinds of jobs people do in the Law & Public Safety pathway. **WoW!**

Some of these job titles will be familiar to you. Others will be so unfamiliar that you will scratch your head and say "huh?"

INVESTIGATOR • Criminal investigator • Criminalist • Criminal justice teacher • Criminal research specialist • Customs and border patrol officer • Customs and border protection officer • Customs inspector • Customs officer • Deputy sheriff • Detective • Detention officer • District attorney • Dog control officer • Drug abuse resistance education officer (DARE) • Emergency communications operator •

EMERGENCY MANAGEMENT COORDINATOR • Emergency medical technician • Emergency preparedness program specialist • Engine boss • **FBI SPECIAL AGENT** • Fire chief • Fire engineer • **FIREFIGHTER** • Firefighter/emergency medical technician • Firefighter/paramedic • Fire marshal • Fire safety inspector • Forensic scientist • Forensic specialist • Forest firefighter • Forest fire warden • Forest patrolman • Forest ranger • Import specialist • Jailer • Judge • Latent fingerprint examiner • Law clerk • Lawyer • Legal secretary • Narcotics investigator • **PARALEGAL** • Parking enforcement officer • Parole officer • **POLICE**

Find a job title that makes you curious. Type the name of the job into your favorite Internet search engine and find out more about the people who have that job.

 What do they do?

Where do they work?

How much training do they need to do this job?

OFFICER • Private investigator • Probation officer • Public defender • Public safety dispatcher • Public safety officer • Retail loss prevention specialist • Security analyst • Security guard • Security manager • Security screener • Shift commander • Sociology professor • **SOCIAL WORKER** • Squad boss • State trooper • Training officer • Transit police officer • Transportation security officer • Wildland firefighter

TAKE YOUR PICK

	Put stars next to your 3 favorite career ideas	Put an X next to the career idea you like the least	Put a question mark next to the career idea you want to learn more about
Attorney			
Crime Scene Investigator			
Emergency Management Coordinator			
FBI Special Agent			
Firefighter			
Paralegal			
Police Officer			
Social Worker			
	What do you like most about these careers?	What is it about this career that doesn't appeal to you?	What do you want to learn about this career? Where can you find answers?
Which Big Wow List ideas are you curious about?			

EXPLORE SOME MORE

The Law & Public Safety pathway is only one of 16 career pathways that hold exciting options for your future. Take a look at the other 15 to figure out where to start exploring next.

Architecture and Construction

WOULD YOU ENJOY making things with LEGOs™, building a treehouse or birdhouse, or designing the world's best skate park?

CAN YOU IMAGINE someday working at a construction site, a design firm, or a building company?

ARE YOU CURIOUS ABOUT what civil engineers, demolition technicians, heavy-equipment operators, landscape architects, or urban planners do?

Arts & Communications

WOULD YOU ENJOY drawing your own cartoons, using your smartphone to make a movie, or writing articles for the student newspaper?

CAN YOU IMAGINE someday working at a Hollywood movie studio, a publishing company, or a television news station?

ARE YOU CURIOUS ABOUT what actors, bloggers, graphic designers, museum curators, or writers do?

Business & Administration

WOULD YOU ENJOY playing Monopoly, being the boss of your favorite club or team, or starting your own business?

CAN YOU IMAGINE someday working at a big corporate headquarters, government agency, or international business center?

ARE YOU CURIOUS ABOUT what brand managers, chief executive officers, e-commerce analysts, entrepreneurs, or purchasing agents do?

Education & Training

WOULD YOU ENJOY babysitting, teaching your grandparents how to use a computer, or running a summer camp for neighbor kids in your backyard?

CAN YOU IMAGINE someday working at a college counseling center, corporate training center, or school?

ARE YOU CURIOUS ABOUT what animal trainers, coaches, college professors, guidance counselors, or principals do?

 Finance

WOULD YOU ENJOY earning and saving money, being the class treasurer, or playing the stock market game?

CAN YOU IMAGINE someday working at an accounting firm, bank, or Wall Street stock exchange?

ARE YOU CURIOUS ABOUT what accountants, bankers, fraud investigators, property managers, or stockbrokers do?

Food & Natural Resources

WOULD YOU ENJOY exploring nature, growing your own garden, or setting up a recycling center at your school?

CAN YOU IMAGINE someday working at a national park, raising crops in a city farm, or studying food in a laboratory?

ARE YOU CURIOUS ABOUT what landscape architects, chefs, food scientists, environmental engineers, or forest rangers do?

Government

WOULD YOU ENJOY reading about U.S. presidents, running for student council, or helping a favorite candidate win an election?

CAN YOU IMAGINE someday working at a chamber of commerce, government agency, or law firm?

ARE YOU CURIOUS about what mayors, customs agents, federal special agents, intelligence analysts, or politicians do?

 Health Sciences

WOULD YOU ENJOY nursing a sick pet back to health, dissecting animals in a science lab, or helping the school coach run a sports clinic?

CAN YOU IMAGINE someday working at a dental office, hospital, or veterinary clinic?

ARE YOU CURIOUS ABOUT what art therapists, doctors, dentists, pharmacists, and veterinarians do?

Hospitality & Tourism

WOULD YOU ENJOY traveling, sightseeing, or meeting people from other countries?

CAN YOU IMAGINE someday working at a convention center, resort, or travel agency?

ARE YOU CURIOUS ABOUT what convention planners, golf pros, tour guides, resort managers, or wedding planners do?

Human Services

WOULD YOU ENJOY showing a new kid around your school, organizing a neighborhood food drive, or being a peer mediator?

CAN YOU IMAGINE someday working at an elder care center, fitness center, or mental health center?

ARE YOU CURIOUS ABOUT what elder care center directors, hairstylists, personal trainers, psychologists, or religious leaders do?

Information Technology

WOULD YOU ENJOY creating your own video game, setting up a Web site, or building your own computer?

CAN YOU IMAGINE someday working at an information technology start-up company, software design firm, or research and development laboratory?

ARE YOU CURIOUS ABOUT what artificial intelligence scientists, big data analysts, computer forensic investigators, software engineers, or video game designers do?

Manufacturing

WOULD YOU ENJOY figuring out how things are made, competing in a robot-building contest, or putting model airplanes together?

CAN YOU IMAGINE someday working at a high-tech manufacturing plant, engineering firm, or global logistics company?

ARE YOU CURIOUS ABOUT what chemical engineers, industrial designers, supply chain managers, robotics technologists, or welders do?

Marketing

WOULD YOU ENJOY keeping up with the latest fashion trends, picking favorite TV commercials during Super Bowl games, or making posters for a favorite school club?

CAN YOU IMAGINE someday working at an advertising agency, corporate marketing department, or retail store?

ARE YOU CURIOUS ABOUT what creative directors, market researchers, media buyers, retail store managers, and social media consultants do?

Science, Technology, Engineering & Mathematics (STEM)

WOULD YOU ENJOY concocting experiments in a science lab, trying out the latest smartphone, or taking advanced math classes?

CAN YOU IMAGINE someday working in a science laboratory, engineering firm, or research and development center?

ARE YOU CURIOUS ABOUT what aeronautical engineers, ecologists, statisticians, oceanographers, or zoologists do?

Transportation

WOULD YOU ENJOY taking pilot or sailing lessons, watching a NASA rocket launch, or helping out in the school carpool lane?

CAN YOU IMAGINE someday working at an airport, mass transit system, or shipping port?

ARE YOU CURIOUS ABOUT what air traffic controllers, flight attendants, logistics planners, surveyors, and traffic engineers do?

MY WoW

I am here.

_____
Name

_____
Grade

_____
School

Who I am.

Make a word collage! Use 5 adjectives to form a picture that describes who you are.

Where I'm going.

The next career pathway I want to explore is

_____

Some things I need to learn first to succeed.

1 _____

2 _____

3 _____

My Career Choice

To get here.

GLOSSARY

attorney
person who has studied the law and is trained to advise people and represent them in court; a lawyer

bar exam
a written test that a person must pass before becoming licensed to practice law as an attorney

chaos
complete and usually noisy disorder

civil rights
the individual rights that all members of a democratic society have to freedom and equal treatment under the law

contract
a legal agreement between people or companies stating what each of them has agreed to do and any amounts of money involved

counterintelligence
an agency that attempts to block an enemy's source of information, trick the enemy, and gather political and military information

crime scene investigator
person who collects, preserves, and processes evidence at the scene of a crime

disaster
an event that causes great damage, loss, or suffering, such as a flood or plane crash

DNA
deoxyribonucleic acid, the molecule that carries genes, found inside the nucleus of cells and often found on evidence left behind by criminals

emergency management coordinator
person who coordinates all activities between an emergency management agency and local emergency response agencies and the general public

FBI special agent
person who works for the Federal Bureau of Investigation (FBI) examining cases and watching, capturing, and arresting criminals who violate federal laws

firefighter
person who fights fires and responds to other emergencies

geriatric
related to the health and care of very old people

law
all the jobs involved in planning, managing, and providing legal services and protections

lawsuit
a legal action brought against a person or a group in a court of law

legal brief
an outline of the main information and arguments of a legal case

mediate
to work with opposing sides in an argument or dispute in order to reach an agreement

negotiation
the process of reaching an agreement by discussing something or making a bargain

paralegal
person with legal training who assists a lawyer

police officer
person whose job is to enforce laws, investigate crimes, and make arrests

public safety
all the jobs involved in protecting the public and keeping them safe

social worker
person who works for a government or private organization that helps people who have financial or family problems

testify
to state what you witnessed or know in a court of law

verdict
the decision of a jury about whether an accused person is guilty or not guilty

INDEX

About the Author

Diane Lindsey Reeves is the author of lots of children's books. She has written several original PEANUTS stories (published by Regnery Kids and Sourcebooks). She is especially curious about what people do and likes to write books that get kids thinking about all the cool things they can be when they grow up. She lives in Cary, North Carolina, and her favorite thing to do is play with her grandkids—Conrad, Evan, Reid, and Hollis Grace.

Since Lacey Reeves was a child she has been watching her mother, Diane Lindsey Reeves, write books. This is the first (and certainly not the last) book they have co-authored together. She is a child life specialist and lives in Charleston, South Carolina where her favorite thing to do is go to the beach with her daughter Hollis Grace.